Developing Citize

ACTIVITIES FOR PERSONAL, SOCIAL AND HEALTH EDUCATION

year

Christine Moorcroft

A & C BLACK

Contents

Reprinted 2007
Published 2005 by A & C Black Publishers Limited
38 Soho Square, London W1D 3HB
www.acblack.com

ISBN 978-0-7136-7120-9

The author and publishers would like to thank Catherine Yemm
and Roy Honeybone for their assistance in producing this book.

Every effort has been made to trace copyright holders and to
obtain permission for use of copyright material. The author and
publishers would be pleased to rectify in future editions any
error or omission.

A CIP catalogue record for this book is available from the
British Library.

Printed in Great Britain by St Edmundsbury Press,
Bury St Edmunds, Suffolk.

A & C Black uses paper produced with elemental chlorine-
free pulp, harvested from managed sustainable forests.

Developing Citizenship is a series of seven photocopiable activity books for citizenship lessons (including Personal, Social and Health Education and, in the foundation stage, *Personal, social and emotional development*). Each book provides a range of activities to help teachers to prepare children to play an active role as citizens, including:

- developing confidence and responsibility, and making the most of their abilities;
- developing a healthy, safe lifestyle;
- developing good relationships and respecting differences between people;
- helping children to think for themselves, to express their own thoughts and opinions confidently, and to learn to listen to others' points of view;
- helping children to become full members of the groups they belong to, knowing they have rights but also becoming increasingly aware of their responsibilities.

The activities in **Year 4** are based on the QCA Scheme of Work for Citizenship at Key Stages 1 and 2 and support children's development in the following areas:

- understanding themselves as individuals and members of their communities;
- learning basic rules and skills for keeping themselves healthy and safe and for behaving well;
- taking responsibility for themselves and their environment;
- understanding their own and other people's feelings;
- awareness of the views, needs and rights of other people;
- social skills such as taking turns, sharing, playing, helping others, resolving simple arguments and resisting bullying;
- participating in the life of their school and neighbourhood.

The activities are linked with other areas of the curriculum where appropriate. Teachers are encouraged to introduce them in a stimulating environment that provides opportunities for the children to develop a sense of responsibility: for example, they can organise equipment and contribute to class decision-making.

Each activity sheet features a **Teachers' note** at the foot of the page, which may be masked before photocopying. Expanded teaching notes are provided in **Notes on the activities** on pages 5–11. Most of the activity sheets end with a challenge (**Now try this!**) which reinforces and extends the children's learning and provides the teacher with an opportunity for assessment. These activities might be appropriate for only a few children; it is not expected that the whole class should complete them. A separate sheet of paper will be needed for some extension activities.

Beyond the classroom

The series takes into account that unplanned experiences which the children have at school and in other places can contribute to the development of concepts and attitudes concerning citizenship. To help teachers to link children's learning through taught activities with their learning at other times, the teachers' notes make suggestions wherever possible for promoting the development of citizenship outside lesson times.

Organisation

The activities require very few resources beyond pencils, scissors, card and other general classroom items. Any other materials you will need are specified in the **Notes on the activities** (for example, computers, information books and leaflets, pictures and storybooks).

Vocabulary

Key vocabulary to be introduced is provided in the **Notes on the activities**.

Health and safety

Developing Citizenship provides advice on how to make lessons safe and how to encourage children to take responsibility for their own safety. Specific health and safety notes are included in the **Notes on the activities** where appropriate. Advice on implementing safe policy and practice for use of the Internet in schools can be found on the British Educational Communications and Technology Agency's website: www.becta.org.uk.

Useful websites

Citizenship education curriculum: www.dfes.gov.uk/citizenship (summarises the citizenship curriculum, offers free resources for teachers, links to the QCA schemes of work)

Citizenship Foundation: www.citizenshipfoundation.org.uk (supports education about the law, democracy and society)

Institute for Citizenship: www.citizen.org.uk/education (ideas for classroom activities; links to websites offering useful information)

Association for Citizenship Teaching: www.teachingcitizenship.org.uk (a professional association for citizenship teachers)

Virtual Teacher Centre: http://curriculum.becta.org.uk/docserver.php?docid=6653 (information and resources for citizenship teachers; links include downloadable lesson plans from the Teacher Resource Exchange)

Community Service Volunteers: www.csv.org.uk (aims to reconnect people to their community through volunteering and training)

Council for Education in World Citizenship: www.cewc.org (aims to involve students, teachers and other citizens in taking responsibility for the world's future)

School Councils UK: www.schoolcouncils.org (advice on how to set up and run school councils)

Personal Finance Education Group: www.pfeg.org (aims to develop financial capability in young people)

4Learning: www.channel4.com/learning/microsites/C/citizenship (citizenship resources and TV listings; links to interactive activities)

Childline: www.childline.co.uk (advice on communication skills and relationships)

Notes on the activities

The notes below expand upon those provided at the foot of each activity page. They give ideas for making the most of the activity sheet, including suggestions for a whole-class introduction, a plenary session or for follow-up work using an adapted version of the activity sheet.

The notes also suggest links which can be made with other areas of the curriculum and ways of developing citizenship through everyday experiences: for example, involving the children in the planning of school events and discussing any problems the school faces and their possible solutions.

To help teachers to select appropriate learning experiences for their pupils, the activities are grouped into sections within each book, but the pages need not be presented in the order in which they appear, unless stated otherwise.

Where appropriate, television programmes, stories, poems or non-fiction sources, such as newspaper reports, Internet articles or advertisements, are suggested for introducing the activities or rounding them off.

Taking part

These activities develop skills of communication, participation in decision-making activities and contribution to school life.

Mime (page 12) develops the children's ability to use non-verbal as well as spoken methods of communicating information. You could show them newspaper pictures and works of art of people expressing emotions: for example, *The Scream* (Edvard Munch), *Hunters in the Snow* (Pieter Brueghel the Elder), *Football Players* (Henri Rousseau), *Pietà* (Ercole de' Roberti), *David Garrick as Richard III* (William Hogarth), *And When Did You Last See Your Father?* (William F Yeames). Cartoons could also be used, since they exaggerate emotions.

> **Vocabulary:** *body language, emotion, express, expression, feeling, mime.*

Budget (page 13) develops the children's skills in working in a group. It can be used at the start of the school year to involve them in the organisation of the classroom. It also encourages them to think in terms of cost. It can be followed up by the activities suggested on pages 14 and 15.

> **Vocabulary:** *advantage, budget, consult, disadvantage, discuss, share.*

Sell your idea (page 14) provides an opportunity for the children to develop skills in presenting ideas in a persuasive way, speaking audibly and clearly and taking into account the needs and interests of their audience. It can be linked with work in literacy (speaking and listening). Encourage them to collect information to support their idea. This can be linked with the activity on page 13 or with other real-life consultation within the class.

> **Vocabulary:** *consult, expression, interest, listen, present.*

Feedback (page 15) helps the children to give and receive constructive feedback. Draw out that criticisms are not personal; they should be about the idea and should help to improve it. They should be thinking about the ideas themselves, rather than who put them forward. The children can give feedback orally. Afterwards, ask them to complete the sheet to evaluate their own presentation. This can be linked with the activities on pages 13 and 14 or with another real-life consultation.

> **Vocabulary:** *evaluate, feedback, improve, negative, positive, presentation.*

Choices

This section provides opportunities for the children to develop an awareness of the choices they can make and how to make the best choices in different situations. The activities can be linked with work in RE on right and wrong and are appropriate for introduction through circle time.

Decision tree (page 16) helps the children to become aware of the processes of decision-making and the strategies they use. Draw out that, even when they know what choice they should make, this might be difficult and there might be reasons why they make the wrong choice. They could also discuss and complete decision trees for people in the news or people from history.

> **Vocabulary:** *choice, consequences, decision, right, wrong.*

No-win situation (page 17) re-tells a well-known fable by Æsop to introduce the idea that some choices people make might be unpopular. You could begin by inviting the children to talk about decisions they have not liked which were made by people such as parents, carers or teachers. Ask them to explain why they think the decisions were made and whether they now agree with them. Why did they not like the decisions at the time? The moral of the fable is 'You can't please everyone'. What does this say about how the behaviour of other people can change or affect decisions? Draw out that people have different views about some issues, but on others there is general agreement.

> **Vocabulary:** *agree, choice, decision, disagree, influence, moral, please, popular.*

Listen to this (page 18) draws out that peer pressure can influence decisions – sometimes for the better. During circle time the children could talk about times when they wanted to influence events but could not or were afraid to try. The pupils could be challenged 'Is it wrong to do/say nothing?' This could be linked with literacy (fiction writing based on experiences and the effects of a character's choice on the outcome of the story). The children could use a word-processor for the extension activity.

> **Vocabulary:** *choice, decision, influence, outcome, pressure.*

Face the facts (page 19) develops the children's ability to distinguish between fact and opinion. They could collect reports from different newspapers about the same events or issues and compare the ways in which they are presented. Encourage them to notice how the writer's choice of language communicates his or her opinion and can be used to try to persuade the reader. This has links with literacy (writing newspaper reports and distinguishing between fact and opinion in texts).

> **Vocabulary:** *communicate, fact, language, opinion, report, view.*

Media matters (page 20) is about the ways in which the media target their audience. Discuss why advertisements are made and whether they make any difference to what people spend their money on. Have the children ever bought something (or asked for it) because of an advertisement? Point out that, by law, advertisers are not allowed to make false claims or suggestions. Other questions for discussion include: 'How does the advertisement work?', 'Is it effective?' and 'Do other people's opinions/ recommendations influence you?' This can be linked with literacy lessons on persuasive texts and writing for an audience.

> **Vocabulary:** *advertisement, audience, claim, layout, media, product, suggestion.*

Animals and us

These activities develop the idea of rights and responsibilities. They draw on the children's learning from **Year 3** on the needs of animals. Help them to find out about dog welfare charities such as Dogs Trust (www.dogstrust.org.uk). Many dog rescue charities are listed on www.dogpages.org.uk. The Kennel Club (www.the-kennel-club.org.uk) provides information about different breeds.

Dog watch (page 21) is about the responsibilities of pet owners. Remind the children of their previous learning about the basic needs of all animals for food, water, air and shelter. Do the children think dogs can feel anger, excitement, fear, happiness or sadness? How can they tell? Children who have dogs could describe how their pets show these feelings. What might make dogs bored? What might they do if they are bored? Dogs can also feel fear; some dogs feel afraid if they are left at home because dogs tend to guard their territory and if everyone goes out they feel that they have a whole house to guard. During the plenary session, point out that it might appear cruel to put a dog in a cage, but that these 'dog crates' can be used for short periods of time (for example an hour or two) where a dog is destructive if bored or afraid, or is not yet house-trained. Also point out that it can be very dangerous to leave a dog in a car in sunny weather because the interior of a car can become very hot in a few minutes and the dog could quickly become dehydrated.

> **Vocabulary:** *anger, boredom, excitement, fear, feelings, happiness, sadness.*

Sad dog stories (page 22) introduces the need for voluntary and charitable organisations which care for animals. A visit from an RSPCA inspector would be valuable or the children could read RSPCA case studies and discuss why people are cruel to dogs. Draw out that some people do not realise that they are treating a dog cruelly; they are ignorant about how to care for it; some do not

know how to socialise it (so that, for example, it is house-trained, does not bite people and does not destroy furniture and clothes); some have difficulties in caring for their dogs (for example, because they are ill); some neglect their pets because they cannot be bothered to provide for their needs or are too busy; others are deliberately cruel. It is illegal to treat animals cruelly and the police have powers to arrest anyone who breaks this law and to take the animals to be cared for by charities. People found guilty of cruelty to animals can be fined or imprisoned.

> **Vocabulary:** *care, cruel, cruelty, neglect.*

Dog rescue (page 23) is about the history and purpose of animal welfare charities. If possible, invite a representative or volunteer from a dog rescue charity to come and talk to the children about its founder, why it was founded and the work it does. They could explain how each dog is treated when it arrives, how it is cared for and re-homed. The children could 'adopt' one of these organisations and find out how they can help it: for example, through organising fund-raising activities.

> **Vocabulary:** *charity, founder, funds, rescue, volunteer.*

Collie care (page 24) is about charities that help particular animals and the importance of careful consideration when choosing a pet. Different breeds of dog have been bred for different purposes and so tend to have particular characteristics and needs. Border collies have been bred for centuries as working farm dogs, usually to herd sheep, because of their natural herding instincts, intelligence, strong gaze, great stamina and willingness to please. They tend to respond to one person only, are very energetic, need a great deal of exercise and mental stimulation and, if bored, look for something to do (if there is nothing else to do they might amuse themselves by chewing furniture). They sometimes try to herd small children, nipping at their ankles as they do so. For these reasons some collies can be difficult pets but, if they are well exercised and given plenty of mental challenges, they can be delightful pets. The children can find out more about Border collies from:
>   www.bordercollierescue.org
>   www.bordercollietrustgb.org.uk
For comparison you could ask the children to find out about another breed.

> **Vocabulary:** *Border collie, breed, characteristics, charity, herding, instinct, nature, rescue, sheepdog.*

A dog's life (page 25) is about the importance of careful consideration when choosing a pet and helps the children to learn what is involved in caring for pets. If possible, invite a dog-handler or trainer to talk about his or her work. Discuss what dogs need to be taught for their own safety and to make them pleasant pets – and what they can be taught for their own and their owners' fun. Draw out that some dogs are also trained as working dogs: sheepdogs, guide dogs, and so on.

> **Vocabulary:** *behaviour, problem, solution, train.*

People who help us – the local police

These activities are about the work of the police and other local organisations, and would be enhanced through contact with the local police's schools liaison officer. The activities develop the children's awareness of the work of the police in keeping the community safe and provide opportunities to explore issues of right and wrong, crimes, penalties and punishments. Local and regional police forces' contact details can be found via links from www.police.uk.

Local trouble (page 26) is about issues that are dealt with by the police and other organisations and draws on the children's previous learning about handling conflict and making decisions. Discuss how the problem presented here might have arisen. Why might these children be causing problems? How can the police officer find out what has been going on and how bad the situation is? The children could list the kinds of evidence that are needed and how it can be collected.

> **Vocabulary:** *problem, solution, trouble, vandalism.*

Talking point (page 27) provides opportunities for the children to explore the ways in which decisions are made by the police or other local organisations. You could begin with news reports about a local problem. Help the children to collect evidence, including the views of the people affected by it. Ask them to describe and then summarise the problem, to say whom it affects, and how, to discuss possible solutions and to make a note of all their ideas before choosing the two they think are the best. Draw out that no solution will be perfect and ask them to consider the advantages and disadvantages of each one. This could be linked with **Decision tree**, page 16. It could also be linked with work in geography on local issues.

> **Vocabulary:** *advantage, disadvantage, issue, problem, solution, views.*

Spot the crimes (page 28) is about the need for the police to protect the community from crime. The ten crimes shown are armed robbery, arson, assault, burglary, car theft, owning a dog which is out of control in a public place, cruelty to animals, mugging (robbery), shoplifting and vandalism. Draw out that, as well as the immediate victims, a crime can affect others: for example, shops have to price goods to cover the losses they face through theft; a dog which is treated cruelly could become vicious; if a car is stolen, its owner might be able to make a claim from an insurance company, but the more car crime there is, the more everyone pays.

> **Vocabulary:** *armed robbery, arson, assault, burglary, car theft, crime, cruelty to animals, mugging, shoplifting, vandalism, victim.*

It's a crime (page 29) is about the work of the police. It focuses on what is meant by 'crime' and encourages the children to consider which crimes are the most serious, and why. They could combine the results of the whole class to create a ladder which represents their collective views. Help them to find out from news reports about the ways in which people are punished for the crimes listed here. Do they think the punishment fits the crime? Is the same punishment always given for the same crime? Should it be? This could be linked with work in RE on rules and laws. Draw out the similarities and differences between the laws of religions and the law of the land.

> **Vocabulary:** *arson, assault, burglary, community service, crime, drug-dealing, fine, fraud, handling, jail, law, murder, punishment, robbery, sentence, serious, shoplifting, vandalism, victim.*

Living in a diverse world

In this section the children learn about identities and communities. The activities develop their understanding of basic human needs and rights, equality among people, respect for themselves and others, membership of communities (including school and family) and the differences and similarities between people.

Community links (page 30) develops the children's understanding of their place within the local community; it provides opportunities for them to discuss and communicate their feelings about their community. They could make a booklet about their local community or create an electronic leaflet which could be linked to the school's website. Maps of the local area will be useful for this activity, which has links with geography (Connecting ourselves to the world; Improving the area we can see from our window); it also links with the ICT curriculum (using e-mail).

> **Vocabulary:** *community, local, special.*

Reaching out (page 31) helps the children to recognise diversity in their community. These websites might help:
> www.mandirnet.org
> www.shopumust.com/pls/public/dir.show?cat_id=1911
> www.theredirectory.org.uk/orgs/ncht.html
> www.rip-il.com/jewish_links_directory_synagogues_uk.asp
> www.findachurch.co.uk
> www.salaam.co.uk/mosques/index.php
> www.sikh.net/Gurdwara/World/GWUK.htm

The children could make a map, based on an Ordnance Survey or street map, on which they mark places connected with different faiths. They could make a calendar of religious festivals and events in the local community. This can be linked with RE (Religions in your neighbourhood) and with geography (Developing mapping skills).

> **Vocabulary:** *church, community, faith, mandir, mosque, religion, synagogue, temple, vihara.*

Small world (page 32) encourages the children to learn about different places and communities through drawing on their own experience and that of others. The activity could be developed during geography lessons. There are also opportunities to link it with history (People who have invaded and settled in Britain – the reasons why people move from the place where they were born). Numeracy skills can be developed if the children use the scales of the maps to help them to calculate how far the people in their survey have travelled from their place of birth.

> **Vocabulary:** *birthplace, community, diverse, diversity, emigrate, immigrate, migrate, settle.*

New arrivals (page 33) helps to develop strategies to deal with prejudice by encouraging the children to welcome new people to their community. It could be used in connection with welcoming new pupils to the school, especially those from different types of community (including refugees and asylum-seekers). Draw out the difference it makes to newcomers if they are made to feel welcome and the way in which this helps to create a pleasant atmosphere in the community.

> **Vocabulary:** *community, immigrant, newcomer, welcome.*

Developing our school grounds

This section involves the children in observation, discussion, problem-solving and co-operation. It develops the ability to work in a democratic way which takes account of the needs and wishes of the whole community. It can be linked with work in geography on the use of maps and plans.

Spot the ball (page 34) helps to develop the children's roles as members of the school community. It can be used to introduce the idea that they can help to solve problems at school, rather than waiting for adults to do so. It has links with geography (Improving the view we can see from our window).

> **Vocabulary:** *community, feature, problem, solution.*

Hot spots (page 35) involves recording features on an outline map. It can be linked with work in geography (Improving the view we can see from our window). Discuss with the children which parts of the playground they think are used the most and the least, and why. Does this cause any problems?

> **Vocabulary:** *features, key.*

Forum and **Action plan** (pages 36–37) encourage the children to consult members of the school community (including different age groups) before considering what could be done to improve the use of the playground. During the plenary session following the first activity, discuss why some parts of the playground are over- or under-used. Ask the children to consider ways of encouraging pupils to make more use of the least popular areas. During another lesson, the children could brainstorm ideas in groups and then consider the advantages and disadvantages of each suggestion before choosing one.

> **Vocabulary:** *brainstorm, consult, survey.*

Costing (page 38) helps the children to learn about the costs and limitations of their plans. The activity could be linked with pages 35–37 or to support work on another project. It develops literacy and research skills as the children use local directories, newspaper advertisements and retailers' brochures and leaflets to find goods and their costs. There are also links with mathematics (adding and subtracting money). Once a project has been agreed, the children could be given a budget. If their costing turns out to be above the limit, help them to find ways of reducing costs.

> **Vocabulary**: *budget, cost.*

Fund-raiser (page 39) helps the children to consider their expectations for change and the complexities of their project. It could be linked with page 38 or with another fund-raising activity (for example, to support a charity – see **Dog rescue**, page 23). Their tasks could include preparing leaflets, posters, tickets, letters, forms and price tags, collecting, storing, pricing and labelling goods for sale and organising the venue.

Health and safety: The organisation of events in which members of the public are invited into the school must conform with the school's health and safety regulations (including fire safety regulations) and local authority guidelines.

> **Vocabulary:** *collect, funds, plan, prepare, task.*

Children's rights – human rights

This section is about human rights and needs. It develops the children's understanding of fairness and justice and the meaning of prejudice. The children learn how the consideration of human rights applies at school and in the neighbourhood. The Children's Rights Alliance for England website – www.crae.org.uk – explains the United Nations Convention on the Rights of the Child and highlights injustices in the treatment of children in the UK.

Mudlarks (page 40) develops the children's understanding of human rights, about the people whose rights are not always upheld, what can happen to such people and how others can help. Draw on the children's knowledge about Victorian times – particularly the lives of poor people. Remind them about their previous learning about people's needs and rights and tell them that they are going to read about some of the people a Victorian researcher, Henry Mayhew, met in London. The children should be able to identify the following human rights which these people were denied: food, clothes, shelter, a home and warmth and (for children) education and people to look after them.

> **Vocabulary:** *education, hardship, needs, poor, poverty, rights, shelter.*

Ideal world and **You're in charge** (pages 41–42) provide opportunities for the children to consider how they would ensure that people's basic needs and rights were upheld if they were a ruler; they also learn about responsibilities. Ask them if they think it is fair that some people have more money than others, bigger and better homes, better quality clothes and a greater choice of food, and so on. Do they want to change this? If so, how? Should helping less fortunate people be voluntary or should everyone be required to do so by law? Does this already happen in any way? This could be linked with the children's learning in RE (for example, the work of religious-based organisations which help people in need, and the use of Zakah – the Islamic welfare due).

> **Vocabulary:** *benefits, charity, needs, responsibility, rights, sharing.*

In the news (page 43) is about fairness. The children consider what should be done when people's actions harm other people, animals or places. Discuss the punishments the people were given and the penalties for different crimes. Do they think these are fair? If not, how would they change them? Discuss how effective the punishments are and whom they will help. What do the children think should be done about the consequences of the crimes? What can be done to help the victims or to put right any damage? Discuss and, if necessary, explain some of the punishments for crimes: for example, community service, fines, imprisonment.

> **Vocabulary:** *arrest, bench, community service, court, crime, effects, fine, guilty, innocent, judge, jury, magistrate, penalty, prison, punishment, verdict, victim.*

Prejudice (page 44) encourages the children to explore issues of prejudice, which are often linked to racism, gender or age bias, religious intolerance, and so on. The second picture is the only one in which there is a legitimate reason for excluding people from an activity because of an issue such as their size (the fairground ride is considered too dangerous for young children). The children might raise the issue of a very small adult who wants to experience the ride. Discuss whether an exception should be made to the rule and, if so, why. Point out that in the middle of the nineteenth century many Irish immigrants arrived in England, particularly in ports. Many English people resented them and refused them lodgings. Nowadays this would be illegal. Also point out that, in the past, employers could specify an age limit and gender when they advertised jobs but that this, too, is now illegal. When discussing the final picture draw out the reasons why some people might be raising objections. How do they know that the asylum-seekers will not be good neighbours? Draw out that they are pre-judging the asylum-seekers and that this is the meaning of prejudice. This activity could lead to work on equal opportunities. You could discuss the school's equal opportunities policy with the children and ask them to identify some of the ways in which it is put into practice.

> **Vocabulary:** *asylum-seeker, equal opportunities, gender, intolerance, prejudice, racism, tolerance.*

Face to face (page 45) is about resolving or avoiding conflict. It provides an opportunity to use drama to explore issues. After the children have completed the activity, ask them what they have learned from it about how to use classroom resources. This could be reinforced during normal classroom activities. Draw attention to examples of behaviour which avoids conflict or ask the children, during circle time, to talk about ways in which they have seen others acting in a way which avoids or resolves conflicts. This work could also be linked with the children's learning about conflicts in history.

> **Vocabulary:** *avoid, behaviour, conflict, resolution, resolve.*

How do rules and laws affect me?

This section introduces the need for rules and laws in a community in order to protect people's rights and develops the children's understanding of democracy. They discuss rules and laws and learn how to make suggestions and changes. This could be connected with the school or class council.

Council choice (page 46) helps the children to learn about democracy. Ask them to consider what each candidate on the sheet says and to decide how helpful he or she would be as a class representative on the school council. The children could carry out an election and record the results on a graph during an ICT lesson. What did the class feel was important in their choice? Draw out why a secret ballot is fair: no one knows for whom each individual voted and they are not likely to be persuaded or bullied into a particular way of voting. This could be used to introduce a real-life election for a class representative on the school council. Begin by asking which children would be interested and then inviting them to speak briefly to the class about why they would like to take on this role. Follow this with a secret ballot.

> **Vocabulary:** *ballot, candidate, council, elect, election, representative, vote.*

Council problem (page 47) develops the children's understanding of democracy. Remind the children that the class representative has been voted into office in a fair, democratic process. Point out that the actions of the chosen representative

might not please everyone, but that they should take into account the views of the majority. Draw out how problems can be solved at school, either through the school council or through other channels. In another lesson, the children could discuss how to solve any existing problem at school.

> **Vocabulary:** *democracy, democratic, election, fair, majority, minority, representative, vote.*

A fizzy question (page 48) develops the children's ability to take turns in discussions. They also learn to accept that different people have different views. Point out that for this type of voting a secret ballot is not necessary – a show of hands is appropriate. After they have played back their recording, discuss how the recording helped them to become aware of the part everyone played in the discussion and how counting the numbers of times people spoke gives a rough idea of how well everyone contributed. As a further extension activity, they could re-play the tape and time each speaker and refine their evaluations on the basis of this. This activity could be developed during literacy lessons (writing arguments).

> **Vocabulary:** *against, agree, debate, disagree, discussion, evaluation, for, vote.*

Rules and reasons (page 49) develops the children's understanding of why rules are made. 'Smile at least once a day' might sound silly to some children, but others might argue for it because it makes the classroom or school a happier place. 'Keep to the left when walking around the school' might seem petty to some children but it could be a sensible safety rule. 'Count to 100 if you step on an ant' might seem a silly waste of time to some children; others might think of it as a good way of making people care for living things. 'Walk to school' sounds like a sensible rule for good health, but not for long distances or along dangerous roads. 'Ask a question every day' could seem silly to some children, if they think of rules as means of controlling behaviour, but others might think it is a good rule because it helps them to learn.

> **Vocabulary:** *disobey, obey, reason, rule.*

Group roles (page 50) encourages the children to take on different types of responsibility. Ask them to consider the skills and talents of the members of their group and what they enjoy doing. Also discuss what should be done if there are some tasks they all want to take on and others that no one wants to do. How can a fair decision be taken? Remind them that fair decisions do not always please everyone but that, once they have agreed on a way of making a decision, they must keep to it. During another lesson, they could carry out the project they have planned. The visitor could be a charity worker, faith representative, policeman or other member of the local community.

> **Vocabulary:** *agree, disagree, project, responsibility, role, skill, task.*

Respect for property

These activities encourage the children to respect shared property, including school property and property belonging to the community, as well as the property of individuals. They learn to consider the consequences of vandalism and theft.

Yours or ours? (page 51) reinforces the children's learning that stealing is wrong; that shared property should be available for all who have a right to use it and that keeping shared property for their own personal use is stealing. Discuss why shared property is sometimes stolen: the people who steal it do not have to break into a place in order to take it; they have a right to use it, but they also have a responsibility to leave it in the same condition for other users. This activity could be linked with a real-life situation if school items have been stolen. Children who have stolen school goods could be encouraged to bring them back by an acknowledgement that sometimes people do not intend to steal things but that once they have taken them away it can be difficult to bring them back. Encourage the return of such items through an 'amnesty' (discuss this with the class).

> **Vocabulary:** *amnesty, consequences, effects, property, steal, theft.*

Mean burglary (page 52) focuses on the consequences of theft for the victims and for the thieves. The children could read about thefts reported in local newspapers and compile a chart on which to record the facts, how the theft affected the victim and how the culprits were punished. They could compare the punishments and discuss how appropriate they were for the crime and for the culprit. If possible, invite a community liaison police officer to talk to the children about the effects of local crimes on victims and about how the culprits are caught and what happens to them. Alternatively, you could invite a representative of Victim Support to talk to the class about his or her work.

> **Vocabulary:** *crime, culprit, fair, feelings, steal, theft, unfair.*

Putting it right (page 53) encourages the children to use their imagination to understand the experiences of others. Discuss why some people damage property when they have nothing to gain from it. Why do they target cemeteries? The children might not be aware of the sadness which the damage of a grave might cause for someone whose father, mother, child or other close relative or friend has died. In some places community service has involved working on tidying up vandalised cemeteries.

> **Vocabulary:** *cemetery, damage, destruction, grave, grief, property, sadness, vandalism.*

It's our street (page 54) encourages the children to respect property in the community. Point out that this is not an exercise in catching vandals, but to find the small ways in which people can care for their surroundings and which, if carried out by everyone, can make a big difference. To illustrate the effects of lack of care, the children could create a large picture of a street and photograph it. Each day they could glue onto it a piece of litter, scribble a small piece of graffiti, and so on. After a week they could photograph it again and compare this with the first photograph. Link this with work in geography on improving the view from the window. Emphasise that the children can contribute to the appearance of their street by taking their litter home, cleaning up after their dogs or by looking after a tub of plants or a patch of their garden. Ask the children about their experiences of neighbourhood watch schemes and how these help them to look after the place where they live. The children could also contact the local police and the council to find out about the major issues in their neighbourhood and what is being done about them.

> **Vocabulary:** *clean, graffiti, litter, tidy, vandalism.*

Think about it (page 55) focuses on the effects of vandalism. Invite feedback about how the children felt at different points in the story. What did they think might have happened to Terry's dad? Draw out that vandalism can have unexpected consequences and that the obvious victims might not be the only ones to suffer. The children who completed the extension activity could comment on the consequences for other people: for example, shock or injury to the train driver and passengers, cost to the rail company, possible criminal proceedings against the vandals, and so on.

> **Vocabulary:** *consequences, damage, feelings, vandalism.*

Local democracy for young citizens

Through these activities the children learn about their local community: its interesting features, how it has changed over time and what makes it unique. The work of the local council and how it serves the community are introduced, offering opportunities to develop an understanding of democracy.

Landmarks and **Past times** (pages 56–57) focus on the locality of the school and what is special about it. Page 56 focuses on the landmarks that are unique to the locality; these need not be about famous or momentous events on a national scale but those which have shaped the history of the local area. Page 57 concentrates on industries which have shaped the area and which might have disappeared. There are links with work in history – on a specific period or for a local study. You could also invite someone to speak to the children about what it was like to work for a past industry. It would be useful to provide old photographs and maps as well as books about the area. The photographs might show the effect a particular industry had on the local land and what stands in its place now.

> **Vocabulary:** *event, landmark, local, special, unique.*

Finding out (page 58) provides an opportunity for the children to work together to pose questions and undertake research and develops their interest and sense of belonging to the local community. It also helps to build links with people from different age groups within the community and can be carried out in conjunction with local studies in history lessons. Before the children write their questions, encourage them to reflect on what they already know about their local community's history and to decide what else they want to know. Discuss the types of questions they can ask and which are suitable for finding different types of information: for example, closed questions to which the response is 'yes', 'no' or a name or date, and open questions for which it is not easy to predict the types of responses. Remind the children that if one of their friends asks a question that they have also written down they should record the answer at the same time instead of asking the same question again later. Before the extension activity, discuss significant local changes, such as the closure of a factory, the building of a bridge or a new factory or changes in roads, and how one change can lead to another.

> **Vocabulary:** *change, closed question, community, interview, local, open question, past.*

Report it (page 59) is about finding out about the place where the children live. It develops their appreciation of the value and unique character of their local community and provides an opportunity for research. They will need local tourism leaflets, old photographs of the area, old newspapers, information books and access to the Internet, the local library and, if possible, a local history society. The children can find out a great deal about shopping, transport and leisure from photographs of streets in the past and from old newspapers.

> **Vocabulary:** *community, local, media, residents.*

In the media – what's the news?

These activities are about the role of the local and national media – newspapers, radio, television, films and the Internet – in communicating topical local and national news. The children develop skills of enquiry and an understanding of the responsibility involved in reporting news. They learn the importance of collecting evidence to support their views. All the work in this unit can be linked with work in literacy lessons on newspaper reports. The children could visit www.childrens-express.org, which gives information on the Children's Express learning through journalism programme for young people aged 8–18.

Factfinder (page 60) develops the children's skills in identifying facts and opinions in a text. Remind them that some opinions are presented as if they are facts: for example, the first sentence in the report, which makes an assertion that there is going to be a boom in tourism in Southport. Ask the children to look for other ways in which the seller uses the article to promote the lake: for example, he suggests the ways in which a buyer could develop it, points out its main selling points and says that it is the town's second biggest tourist attraction. Discuss how potential purchasers could check these claims, the evidence they could look for and where. Ask the children to identify points made by other people which suggest that buyers need to be cautious about their plans. Is the article balanced? Note that the points made by the local council member are much less prominent and reported in a less exciting way than those of the seller. This can be linked with literacy work on newspaper reports and persuasive texts.

> **Vocabulary:** *attraction, claim, evidence, potential.*

All sides of the story (page 61) encourages the children to evaluate the ways in which the media present information. Discuss whether the same facts are given in each report. Are some omitted or are conflicting facts given? Why? Was one story written at a different time? Had new facts emerged? Discuss why certain facts might be omitted. Explain *bias*. Draw attention to the language used: for example, strong, expressive verbs and adjectives, comparisons, metaphors and similes. What effects are created by the choices of words? Discuss the connotations of words used in the reports.

> **Vocabulary:** *bias, comparison, connotation, expressive, language, metaphor, simile.*

A safe place to cross (page 62) provides an opportunity to investigate local issues. It can be carried out in conjunction with geography lessons on local issues (*Improving the environment; What's in the news?*). The children could read reports about traffic management strategies. They could write to Transport 2000 (the National Environmental Transport Campaign) for information about their schemes and even take part in one of the competitions to find the worst example in Britain of a specific traffic problem. Through Transport 2000 they could find out about traffic issues around Britain. Transport 2000 publishes a monthly report (*Transport Retort*) and can be contacted at Transport 2000, The Impact Centre, 12–18 Hoxton Street, London N1 6NG, Tel 020 7613 0743, Fax 020 7613 5280, e-mail steveh@transport2000.org.uk, website www.transport2000.org.uk. The children could hold their own mini-competition to find the worst road to cross in their locality. Each group could nominate a road to investigate, plan an investigation and collect evidence, such as how long people have to wait before they can cross the road (see **Facts and figures**, page 63), what help exists for pedestrians and how far out of their way some pedestrians have to go to find a safe place to cross.

Health and safety: Before off-site visits, a risk assessment should be carried out. Encourage the children to contribute to the safety rules for the outing.

> **Vocabulary:** *campaign, evidence, issue, local, problem, research, solution, survey, traffic, transport.*

Facts and figures (page 63) develops the children's skills in planning an enquiry about a local issue. They use and develop mathematical skills as they make a careful record of the evidence they collect about a traffic problem. Draw out that in a democratic system, anyone who has a problem concerning any aspect of life in the community can ask their elected local council to consider it; it is useful if they first collect evidence. Point out that evidence in the form of recorded facts is more useful than vague descriptions such as *We can never cross the road*, *Sometimes we wait for ages* or *It's dangerous*. Point out that a useful type of evidence for comparisons is the time it takes people to cross the road.

Health and safety: Before off-site visits, a risk assessment should be carried out. Supervision is essential for this investigation.

> **Vocabulary:** *dangerous, democratic, elected, evidence, issue, observe, problem, record.*

Front page (page 64) provides an opportunity for the children to learn about how to present information. It can be linked with work in literacy lessons on writing non-fiction texts modelled on those they have read. Encourage them to model their writing on the style of newspaper reports and to consider the choice of information that readers will want. They could look at headlines and opening sentences of newspaper reports to learn about the ways in which newspaper reporters attract the attention and interest of their readers. The finished reports could be used to form a display: the children could do a first draft on this sheet and then produce a final version on the computer using a newspaper program. They could add a photograph of the road if the school has a digital camera.

> **Vocabulary:** *article, balance, bias, byline, fact, headline, media, newspaper, opinion, paragraph, report.*

Mime

- **Work with a partner.**
- **Choose a scene to mime.**
- **Ask your partner to guess which scene it is.**
- **Then swap roles.**
- **Repeat with a different scene.**

Think about ...

... how the character feels

... how to show those feelings using your
  – face
  – hands and arms
  – body.

1 This girl in a developing country has just walked a very long way to fetch water for her family.	**2** This runner has just won an Olympic gold medal.
3 This girl has just lost her purse. She had saved up for weeks to buy something special.	**4** The final whistle has gone at the end of a football match and this boy is in the losing team.
5 This girl's mother has just told her that she is not allowed out with her friends.	**6** This boy has just been told a very funny joke.
7 This girl has just heard that an alien spaceship has landed in her town.	**8** This woman is weeding the garden and has just picked up something wet and slimy.

Now try this!

- **Cut out six newspaper headlines.**
- **Mime the feelings of the people in one of the stories.**
- **Ask your partner to guess which story it is.**

Teachers' note Ask the children to read each scene and think about how each person feels. How might they show their feelings? Ask the children to imagine they are communicating these feelings on television with the sound turned off. They could also make up other scenes and write them on a blank copy of the grid.

Developing Citizenship
Year 4
© A & C BLACK

Budget

If your class had **£50**, how would you spend it?

> £50 is the budget for a school year.

- **Work in a group of four.**
- **Each write your idea on a banner.**

1

2

3

4

- **Discuss your ideas.**
- **Explain them to the group.**

Now try this!

- **Think about the advantages and disadvantages of each idea.**
- **List them on a chart.**

Idea	Advantages	Disadvantages
1		
2		
3		

Teachers' note This could be used in connection with a real budget or consumable classroom resources could be allocated a value and linked with imitation money or tokens to encourage the children to take responsibility for using resources carefully.

Developing Citizenship
Year 4
© A & C BLACK

Sell your idea

How will you show that your idea is good?

• **Plan a presentation to the class.**

How will you gain your audience's interest?

Introduction

Points to emphasise	Preparing for criticism

Expressing ideas

Face	Hands	Body

Useful props

Pictures	Evidence from research

Conclusion

Now try this!

How would you change this to present it to your headteacher?

• **List two or three ideas.**

Teachers' note This can be used with page 13. Encourage the children to consider their idea for spending the £50 budget and to think of a way of promoting it to the class. They should consider the way in which they speak (choice of words, expression, and so on) and the ways in which they can use body language to present their ideas.

Developing Citizenship
Year 4
© **A & C BLACK**

Feedback

What do your group think about your idea?
- **Record their feedback on this chart.**

My idea

Feedback about my idea

Positive	Negative

Feedback about my presentation

What I did well	What I could do better

- **Write an evaluation of your idea.**
- **Use your notes to help.**

Teachers' note This can be used with pages 13 and 14 or in connection with any activities involving consultation among the children. Encourage them to listen to the person speaking and to make a note of the good points about the idea being presented; they should also make a note of any negative points they think of. Encourage them to consider how to present negative points (see **Notes on the activities**, page 5).

Developing Citizenship
Year 4
© **A & C BLACK**

Decision tree

What might James think about?

- **Write on the decision tree.**

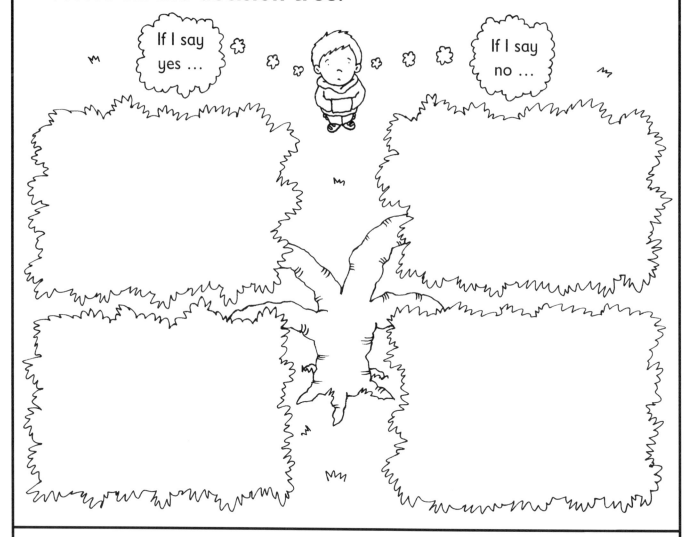

- **Draw a decision tree for a difficult decision you have made.**

Teachers' note Point out that decisions can be difficult even if we know what the right decision is. Discuss the factors that influence a decision: effects on ourselves and others, effects on friendships. Also draw out the possible consequences.

Developing Citizenship
Year 4
© A & C BLACK

No-win situation

What does this story tell you about influences on decisions?

- **Underline the key words and phrases.**

The Man, the Boy and the Donkey

One day a man and his son were walking to the market with their donkey. A man said, 'You fools, why are you walking when you have a donkey?'

So the man put the boy on the donkey and they went on their way. Another man said, 'What a lazy boy to let your father walk while you ride.'

So the son got off the donkey and his father got on.

Before long they passed a woman who said, 'What a cruel man to let your poor little son walk.'

The man wondered what to do.

Then he had an idea. He told his son to get up with him. When they reached the town a woman said, 'How cruel. You two are much too heavy for that poor donkey.'

So they got off the donkey and wondered what to do. They had an idea. They tied the donkey's feet to a pole, rested the pole on their shoulders and carried the donkey. Everyone laughed.

When they came to a bridge the donkey kicked one of its feet loose. It made the boy drop his end of the pole. In the struggle the donkey fell over the bridge into the river. His front legs were tied together, so he couldn't swim and he drowned.

'That will teach you,' said an old man who had followed them.

- **Write the moral of the story.**

_____

Now try this!

- **Write a letter to the old man and his son.**
- **Give them advice about making decisions.**

Teachers' note Tell the children that the story they are going to read is one of Æsop's fables; Æsop was an Ancient Greek writer who wrote stories which were intended to teach people. Ask them to think about what this story was meant to teach the audience and to make notes about the factors that influenced the man and his son. They could write these on a 'decision tree' (see page 16).

Developing Citizenship
Year 4
© A & C BLACK

What good advice could Isla give to her friends?

Think about …   … the consequences   … what she could say.

- **Write in the speech bubbles.**

I found this in our garage. It smells good.

Isla

No one will notice if we go to the shops at playtime.

Quick. Cross here. There's nothing coming.

I'm fed up with Sarah. Don't let her play.

Sarah

Amy   Jack

Now try this!

- **Write the story of one of the pictures.**
- **Write two different endings – make one happy and one sad.**

Teachers' note Ask the children to think about times when friends have given them good advice or made suggestions which helped them to make a good choice. Did they want to listen to their friends? Did they follow their friends' advice? Are they glad they did so? Ask them why. (Focus on the consequences of their actions.)

Developing Citizenship
Year 4
© **A & C BLACK**

Face the facts

- **Read the stories with a partner.**
- **Underline the │facts│ in green.**
- **Underline the │opinions│ in red.**

EYESORE

Residents of Green Road could soon be rid of the ugly piece of waste ground between the school and the post office. The dangerous, rubble-strewn area – home to weeds such as thistles and dock and vermin such as rats and mice – has ruined the outlook of homes facing it for almost ten years. The house which once stood there was burned down and untidy scraps of wallpaper hang from the decaying plaster which clings to the walls of the neighbouring buildings. Children are scared by bats flapping about at night and roosting on bits of rotting wood protruding from the crumbling walls.

Phil Ittin, aged 69, of number 64, said, 'They should bring in the bulldozers as soon as possible. There could be a nice little garden there or even another house.'

Betta Price, 37, agreed: 'The value of our homes has been brought down by that mess. It's a disgrace. And it's unhygienic. I've even seen rats and foxes in there.'

Residents have petitioned the council to clean up this eyesore.

Wonderland

A fascinating wildlife habitat can be found on your doorstep if you are lucky enough to live in Green Road. In a gap between two buildings a past fire has encouraged the growth of lovely pink rose-bay willow-herb (fireweed). Numerous other plants have grown unchecked and they provide a haven for insects, small mammals and birds. The buddleia bushes attract numerous species of butterfly, creating a beautiful colourful display in the summer. In the autumn and winter colour is provided by the cotoneaster bushes which have grown from the droppings of birds which have eaten the berries else-where.

Hans Off, 26, of number 30, hopes that other plants can be encouraged to grow there: 'Some trees have begun to take root. There are a couple of sycamore saplings in which birds will eventually be able to nest.'

Petal Gard, 79, agrees: 'It's good to see nature in the city. I love the surprises I see each season as some-thing new takes root or makes its home here. We must cherish it.'

Nature-lovers have asked a local conservation society to protect the site.

Now try this!

- **Write a summary of the opinions of the two writers.**

Teachers' note Point out that sometimes opinions are expressed as if they are facts: for example, 'The best football team in the world is Liverpool FC', 'Children should be seen and not heard'.

Developing Citizenship Year 4
© A & C BLACK

Media matters

- **Look at an advertisement.**
- **Think about what it is trying to do.**

Product (what the advertisement is for)

Audience (age, gender, interests)	**How I can tell**

How it attracts attention

Pictures	Language	Layout

What it suggests will happen if you buy the product

Now try this!

- **Write about something you bought, or asked for, because of an advertisement.**

What made you want it?

Teachers' note Prepare for this by collecting advertisements from magazines, comics and newspapers. Ask the children to choose an advertisement and to notice how it affects them or how it might affect another type of reader. Draw attention to the product advertised, pictures, style and layout (including flashes, banners, colours, font sizes and styles, and so on). Ask the children to look for any claims it makes: for example, you will become clever, fashionable, popular.

Developing Citizenship Year 4 © **A & C BLACK**

Dog watch

Are these dogs safe and comfortable? ✔ or ✗

- **Explain your answers on the notepads.**

Think about temperature, water and feelings.

Teachers' note Ask the children what dog-owners should do when they have to leave their dogs for different reasons: when they go to work or school, away for a holiday or shopping, or when they take their dog out but it is not allowed into places such as restaurants or shops. Discuss the need for exercise, company and something to do, as well as food and water.

Developing Citizenship Year 4
© A & C BLACK

21

- **Write three things you should do to make sure your dog is safe before you leave it alone.**

Sad dog stories

- ## Discuss these stories with a partner. Write notes about what should be done.

What should be done		
to help this dog	to protect other dogs	about the people who did it
1		
2		
3		

1. Lara is a Labrador puppy, aged 10 months. Neighbours noticed that Lara was very thin and had no energy. They reported her to the RSPCA because they thought her nineteen-year-old owner was not feeding her properly.

2. Jake is a boxer. He was found chained to a fence and covered with wounds, as if he had been whipped. He growled at anyone who went near him.

3. Ella is a cross-breed. Neighbours reported that she was never allowed indoors, even in frosty weather. She slept outdoors without any shelter. Her owners said she could not be trusted indoors; she was destructive and not house-trained.

Now try this!

- ## Find out what happens when someone reports cruelty to a dog.

Teachers' note Read the stories with the children and ask them why the people in each story might have mistreated the dog: for example, they might not have known how to look after it, they might have been busy or they might have been concerned more with enjoying themselves. Should these people have had dogs? What could be done to help them to look after them?

Developing Citizenship
Year 4
© A & C BLACK

Dog rescue

- **Find out about a dog rescue charity.**

You could use the Internet.

Name of charity _____

Address _____

_____

_____

Phone number _____ Fax number _____

E-mail address _____

Website _____

Founder(s)	Date founded
_____	_____

What the charity does when a new dog arrives

_____

_____

_____

_____

_____

_____

_____

_____

_____

_____

- **Find out how the charity finds the dogs new homes.**

Now try this!

- **Write a report about how the charity makes sure that dogs go to good homes.**

Teachers' note Collect information about a dog rescue charity (for example, a locally-based one or one of the many that rescue different breeds or that specialise in a particular breed). You could bookmark its website or send for leaflets and other information about the charity's aims and activities.

Developing Citizenship Year 4
© A & C BLACK

Collie care

There are charities which rescue Border collies only.

- **Find out what is special about this breed.**

Useful websites
www.bordercollierescue.org
www.bordercollietrustgb.org.uk
www.the-kennel-club.org.uk

Purpose for which it was bred	Natural instincts
Characteristics and appearance	**Nature**
Possible problems as a pet	**How to make it a happy pet**

Now try this!

- **Write a letter to someone who wants a Border collie as a pet.**
- **Include all the points you think are important.**

Teachers' note Discuss why some dog rescue charities focus on only one breed (see **Notes on the activities**, page 6) and what distinguishes Border collies from other dogs. The children will need access to information books, leaflets and websites about this breed. Tell them that collies can be difficult to handle as pets because of their natural instincts and, because of this, they are abandoned or given to dog rescue organisations.

Developing Citizenship
Year 4
© **A & C BLACK**

A dog's life

How could these dog-owners solve their problems?

- **Work with a partner.**
- **Write your ideas on the chart.**

Use information books, CDs, DVDs, videos or the Internet.

Scamp chases bikes.

Jess chews shoes.

Possible solutions	Possible solutions
_____	_____
_____	_____
_____	_____
_____	_____
_____	_____
_____	_____
_____	_____

The best solution

_____

_____

The best solution

_____

_____

Now try this!

- **Write instructions to help a dog-owner train a dog to come when it is called.**

Teachers' note Provide information books and leaflets about dog training and access to the websites mentioned in the **Notes on the activities** (see page 6). Ask the children to scan these resources to find the parts that will help to answer their questions. They could use Post-it notes to mark relevant sections of printed material and they could bookmark web pages.

Developing Citizenship
Year 4
© A & C BLACK

Local trouble

- **Discuss this scene with your group.**

These children are a menace. They make life a misery for us.

They terrorise us and are turning the neighbourhood into a slum.

What questions might the police officer ask?

- **Write in the speech bubbles.**

What might the children be doing to annoy people?

- **Write a list.**

_____   _____

_____   _____

_____   _____

Now try this!

- **Think of some reasons why the children might behave like this.**

  What could be done to solve the problem?

- **Discuss this with a partner.**

Teachers' note Ask the children for feedback after they have discussed the scene in their groups. What problem can they identify? Who are causing the problem? What information is needed before the police officer can help the people involved to solve the problem? Draw out the need for details: the people do not say exactly what the children are doing, when and how often.

Developing Citizenship
Year 4
© **A & C BLACK**

Talking point

- **Think about a problem involving children in your local community.**
- **Discuss some solutions. Write about two solutions.**

Problem	People affected
Solution 1	**Solution 2**

Advantages	Disadvantages	Advantages	Disadvantages

- **Write a letter to your local council.**
- **Describe the problem and suggest some solutions.**

Now try this!

Teachers' note Use this page to help the children to organise their findings about a local issue (see **Notes on the activities**, page 7): for example, a traffic problem, a dangerous road or pond, vandalism or other nuisance.

Developing Citizenship
Year 4
© A & C BLACK

Spot the crimes

- **Circle the ten crimes in this picture.**
- **List them on the back of this page.**
- **List the victims of the crimes.**

Now try this!

- **Choose two crimes.**
- **Find out more about them.**
- **Write a report about what happens to people who commit these crimes.**

Teachers' note Ask the children if they think there is a difference between doing wrong and committing a crime. Draw out that a crime is something which is against the law and that people who pcommit crimes are usually punished in some way. Also draw out that there are usually victims, and discuss how they might be affected by crimes. For the extension activity, provide newspaper cuttings about crimes.

Developing Citizenship
Year 4
© A & C BLACK

It's a crime

- **Work in a group.**
- **Cut out the crime cards.**
- **Spread them face up on a table.**
- **Take turns to place a card on the ladder.**
- **Say why you have placed it on that rung.**

Use a dictionary to check the meanings.

Most serious

arson	assault
burglary	drug-dealing
fraud	handling stolen goods
murder	robbery
shoplifting	vandalism

Least serious

Now try this!

- **Read a newspaper report about a crime.**
- **Write notes about how it affected the victims.**

Teachers' note Before the children cut out the crime cards, invite volunteers to explain what each word for a crime means. Tell them that they can move the crimes that have already been placed on the ladder up or down one place in order to make space for the one they want to add. When all the cards have been placed on the ladder the children could continue to take turns to move their positions, each time justifying the move. Afterwards, invite feedback from each group.

Developing Citizenship Year 4
© **A & C BLACK**

Community links

- **Work in a group of five.**
- **Discuss what is special about your local community.**
- **Complete the chart.**

You need e-mail links with another school.

Physical features 	Human features 

Events 	Customs 	People

- **Choose the most important item from one box.**
- **Prepare an e-mail attachment about it.**
- **Send it to your partner school.**

Use sound and pictures as well as text.

Now try this!

- **List three ways in which the other community is similar to yours and three ways in which it is different.**

Teachers' note It is useful to take the children for a walk around the locality of the school before they begin this activity. Encourage them to observe, using all appropriate senses, and to talk about the observations they find the most interesting. Help them to notice the features that make the local area distinctive. Back at school encourage them to talk about interesting local events, customs and people; this could be based on leaflets and local newspapers.

Developing Citizenship
Year 4
© **A & C BLACK**

Reaching out

What can you find out about different religions in your local community?

- Make notes about the evidence you find from:

Ordnance Survey maps

_____
_____
_____
_____
_____
_____
_____

Classified directories

_____
_____
_____
_____
_____
_____
_____

The Internet

_____
_____
_____
_____
_____
_____
_____
_____

People

_____
_____
_____
_____
_____
_____
_____
_____

Now try this!

- Collect information about local religions from other sources:

| posters | buildings | newspapers | signs |

Teachers' note Prepare for this activity by collecting sources from which the children can find out about the different faith groups in their locality: for example, Ordnance Survey maps, street maps and classified directories. You could also invite people from different faiths to talk to the children or to supply information about the locations of their places of worship or other meeting places. It is also useful to bookmark websites (see **Notes on the activities**, page 7).

Developing Citizenship
Year 4
© A & C BLACK

Small world

- **Carry out a survey of the people in your community. Where do they come from?**

I was born here but my Mum came from London.

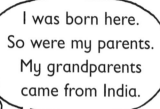

I was born here. So were my parents. My grandparents came from India.

I came from Croatia.

- **Record your results on the chart.**

Name	Place of birth	Parents' birthplaces	Grandparents' birthplaces

Now try this!

- **Find out what drew some people to your local community.**

Teachers' note Prepare for this activity by asking friends of, or visitors to, the school if they will answer the children's questions. You could arrange for this to be carried out through various communication media: letter, fax, e-mail or telephone. Different groups of children could question different people. Before they begin, ask the children to prepare the questions they will ask in order to collect the information they want for their survey.

**Developing Citizenship
Year 4**
© **A & C BLACK**

New arrivals

How can you welcome newcomers to your community?

- **Discuss this with your group.**
- **Write your ideas on the spider chart.**
- **Add two headings of your own.**

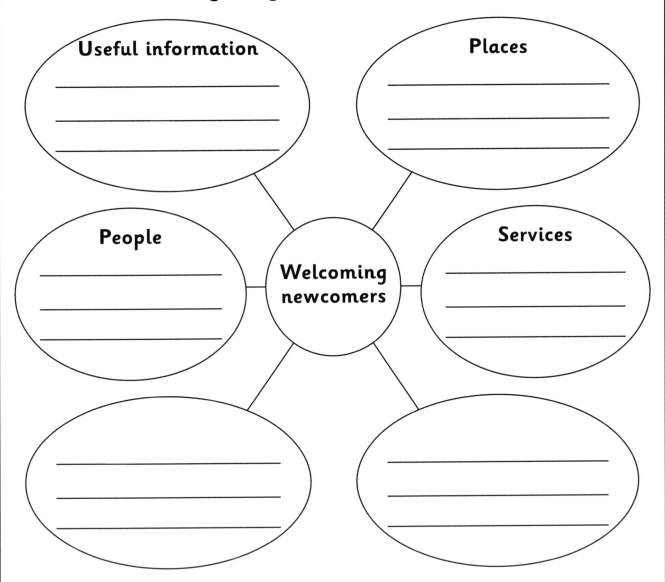

Useful information

Places

People

Welcoming newcomers

Services

- **Plan a booklet to welcome newcomers.**

- **List any problems that newcomers might face.**
- **Evaluate the plan for your booklet.**

  How well does it help to solve each problem?

Teachers' note During circle time, ask the children if they have experiences of moving home. How did they feel? Discuss any problems they faced (such as not knowing their way around and not knowing where to find useful places such as libraries) and who and what helped them to settle in. When they have planned their booklet, different children could work on different sections of it.

Developing Citizenship
Year 4
© **A & C BLACK**

Spot the ball

The children at this school enjoy ball games, but they lose about ten balls every week.

Why is this?

- **In the labels, write notes about the problems of playing ball games.**
- **Link the labels to the balls.**

Now try this!

What could be done to solve the problem of lost balls?

- **Write a letter to the school's headteacher to explain your ideas.**

Teachers' note Tell the children that they are going to find out about a problem faced by a school and to consider what is causing the problem. Afterwards they could make notes about a problem they face at playtime (using annotated drawings, if this helps) and decide what factors are causing it. Point out that sometimes a problem has more than one cause and that it is useful to keep searching even if one cause has been identified.

Developing Citizenship
Year 4
© A & C BLACK

Hot spots

Which parts of the playground do you think are the busiest?

_____

_____

- **Find out.**
- **Draw a map of your playground.**
- **Complete the key. Use colours.**
- **Mark the busiest places ✗.**

Date _____

Key

| | grass | | hard surface | | tree |

How will the 'hot spots' change during the year, and why?

- **Write an explanation.**

Teachers' note Before the children complete this page, ask them to notice in which parts of the playground most children play. Afterwards, discuss whether this will be the same at different times of the year. Ask them to notice whether there are any parts of the playground that are not used at all. This activity could be repeated at different times of the year.

Developing Citizenship
Year 4
© **A & C BLACK**

Forum

Why are some parts of the playground used more than others?

- **Carry out a survey with your group.**
- **Write two questions to ask children.**

    1 _____

    2 _____

- **Record the results on this chart.**

Part of playground	Number who like it the best	Reasons

Now try this!

- **Discuss your conclusions with your group.**
- **Write a summary of your results.**

Teachers' note This can be used with page 35 or another survey on playground use. Explain to the children that a forum is a setting where discussions take place and is a Latin word for a marketplace or a place where public business was conducted. Discuss the questions they need to ask to find the information they need. Different groups of children could focus on different year groups to find answers to their questions.

**Developing Citizenship
Year 4**
© **A & C BLACK**

Action plan

- **Work with a group.**
- **List the two most popular parts of the playground.**

    1 _____   2 _____

- **List the two least popular parts.**

    1 _____   2 _____

- **Explain why some parts are used more than others.**

    _____

    _____

    What could be done to improve the use of the space?

- **List your group's ideas.**

    _____

    _____

    _____

    _____

    _____

    _____

    _____

    _____

- **Write another question that will help you to suggest how to improve the playground.**

Teachers' note This page requires a commitment on the part of the school to involving the children in some aspects of planning. It can be used with pages 35 and 36 or for another project on which the children have agreed. Ask them to notice what happens at playtime and to consider what might encourage better use of the space. Encourage them to think of ideas which involve fairly small changes.

Developing Citizenship
Year 4
© A & C BLACK

Costing

- ## Describe your plan.

_____

_____

_____

- ## List everything you will need.

How much …

- ## Note down where you can buy these things.

- ## Find out the costs.

What we need	Where we can buy it	Cost
		Total cost

What changes could you make to save money?

- ## List your ideas.

Teachers' note This can be used with pages 35–37 or to support another project on which the children have agreed and for which the school is prepared to involve the children to some extent in planning and effecting change. Point out that if they want their plan to be considered by the school staff and governors (perhaps through the school council) they need to have an idea how much it will cost.

Developing Citizenship
Year 4
© A & C BLACK

Fund-raiser

- **Discuss your fund-raising scheme with your group.**
- **Use this page to plan your scheme.**

Our idea

Date(s) and time(s)	Place(s)

People	Tasks	When

What we need to collect or prepare

- **Evaluate your fund-raising scheme.**

  What changes would you make if you repeated it?

Teachers' note This can be used with pages 35–38 or to support another project on which the children have agreed. Afterwards, you could ask the children to evaluate their discussion. Did everyone have a chance to speak? Did they listen to one another? Will everyone have an opportunity to take part in the fund-raising activity?

Developing Citizenship
Year 4
© **A & C BLACK**

Mudlarks

What rights do you think all children have?

- **Make a list.**

Children's rights

to have food, to _____

_____

Which of these rights are being kept from the children in the report?

- **Circle the key words and phrases.**

He wore tattered old rags, stiffened with mud. It was difficult to tell from what kind of material they were made or what colour they had been. His feet were bare. He had a pair of shoes once, he said. He didn't mind much being soaked with mud in the summer but it was very cold in winter.

He was twelve years old. His father was dead and his mother worked when she could – cleaning or washing. She had a shilling* a day. Some days he earned a penny by selling the scraps of objects he found in the mud: nails, rope and anything which was thrown overboard from the ships. 'Mudlarks' they were called – these wretched children. Some were only six years old. As soon as the tide was low enough they scrambled down the steps and waded, sometimes waist-deep, through the filth and mud, pulling out anything they could sell.

He had been to school for a month before he went mudlarking. He could neither read nor write. He did not think he could, even if he 'tried ever so much'. He didn't know what religion his mother was. His mother did not go to church and neither did he, for 'we have no clothes'.

All the money he had, he gave to his mother and she bought bread. The rest of the time they lived the best way they could.

He was more fortunate than some, who had no homes. They slept wherever they could find shelter.

* shilling – 12 pence (an old penny was about half the value of a modern penny)

This extract is based on a true report written in the 1860s by Henry Mayhew.

Now try this!

- **Find out about poor children from Victorian times who did other work.**

What rights were being kept from them?

- **Write a report about them.**

Teachers' note Tell the children that Henry Mayhew wrote reports about poor people, some of whom he interviewed, in London in the middle of the nineteenth century. Ask the children if they think there are people as poor as this in Britain nowadays. Invite them to share their lists of the rights they think all children have. What do they think should have been done to help the children in the report?

Developing Citizenship
Year 4
© A & C BLACK

Ideal world

- **Invent an ideal world where people have everything they need and all their rights.**

- **Make notes about your ideal world.**

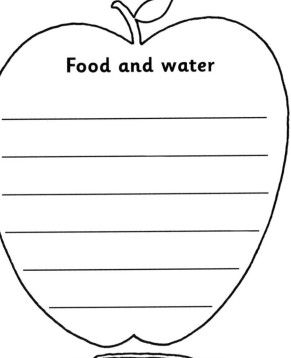

Food and water

_____
_____
_____
_____
_____

Homes

_____
_____
_____
_____
_____

Clothes

_____
_____
_____
_____
_____

Keeping warm

_____
_____
_____
_____
_____

Now try this!

- **Think about two other rights people have.**

- **Describe how your ideal world provides these rights for everyone.**

Teachers' note Ask the children to identify the needs and rights everyone has. In a perfect country everyone would have all he or she needed and all his or her rights. Discuss anything they think is unfair about life in their own country. Invite them to talk about their ideas of a perfect country.

Developing Citizenship Year 4 © A & C BLACK

You're in charge

- **Imagine you are the ruler of a country. What laws would you make so that all people were given their needs and rights?**
- **Discuss this with a partner.**
- **Write notes.**

Word bank

comfort
enough
food
freedom
hardship
home
poor
poverty
shelter
tax
water

Notes

_____

_____

_____

_____

- **List the five most important laws you would make.**

1 _____

_____

2 _____

_____

3 _____

_____

4 _____

_____

5 _____

_____

Now try this!

Why do you think some people are denied their rights?
- **Write an explanation.**

Teachers' note Remind the children about their previous work on human needs and rights. Can they think of groups of people whose needs and rights are not always met, and why? Encourage them to talk about what they would do if they were the leader of their own country. What would they change in order to give everyone his or her rights?

Developing Citizenship
Year 4
© A & C BLACK

In the news

- **Work with a group.**
- **Discuss a news report in which people did wrong.**
- **Write about it on the chart.**

Headline

Summary

List the main points.

People who did wrong	What they did

People, animals or places their actions affected	How they affected them
	How they were punished

Now try this!

- **What should be done to help the victims?**
- **Write a letter to the newspaper.**

Teachers' note Prepare for this activity by collecting appropriate news items (from the radio, television, newspapers or the Internet). Ask the children to identify the people in the report who did wrong. How were they punished? Discuss whether the punishments were fair.

**Developing Citizenship
Year 4**
© A & C BLACK

Prejudice

Is prejudice being shown? Yes or No

- **Explain your answers.**

Green St. Liverpool ROOMS TO LET NO IRISH call 897212 TO LET call 7362 ...niture	[ ] because _____ _____ _____ _____
ROLLER COASTER ← YOU MUST BE AT LEAST THIS HEIGHT TO RIDE!	[ ] because _____ _____ _____ _____
WANTED CAR SALESMAN TO PROMOTE NEW RANGE EXPERIENCE ESSENTIAL AGE 25-35	[ ] because _____ _____ _____ _____
SAY 'NO' TO ASYLUM SEEKERS' HOSTEL IN SMALLTOWN SAY NO TO SEEKERS IN ...AY NO!	[ ] because _____ _____ _____ _____

Now try this!

- **Choose one example of prejudice.**

  What do you think made the people prejudiced?

- **Write an explanation.**

Teachers' note Ask the children to give some examples of prejudice and to explain what they think it means. Draw out that it means 'pre-judging': that is, forming an opinion about someone or something without knowing much about him, her or it. Prejudice usually excludes people because others make a judgment about them based on one or a few facts: for example, their age, gender, race or religion.

Developing Citizenship Year 4
© **A & C BLACK**

Face to face

- **Discuss the pictures with a partner.**

- **Draw what might happen next.**
- **Include speech bubbles.**

Why do you think there was a conflict?

_____

_____

What could have been done to avoid the conflict?

_____

_____

- **Act out what could have been done.**

Who can help to resolve the conflict in the pictures? How?
- **Write your ideas.**

Teachers' note Invite feedback after the children have discussed the pictures in their groups. How could both the girls and the boys in the pictures have acted which would have avoided the conflict? Draw out that the girls had a greater need for the large table than the boys but that the boys would have been more likely to move to another table if the girls had approached them differently. The children could enact this, showing how the conflict could have been avoided.

Developing Citizenship
Year 4
© **A & C BLACK**

Council choice

These children have offered to be the school council representative for their class.

Josie

I think it is important that girls have equal opportunities in the playground. We should have a few quiet areas with benches.

William

We need to stop all bullying. There isn't much of it in our school but we have to make sure it doesn't happen. I'd like to see a 'bully watch' scheme.

May

I want us to have after-school clubs for things like art, science, chess and dancing. There isn't much to do after school.

Salim

I think I'd be good at listening to what children in the class want. I'd just like to make sure everything is fair.

Hannah

I've won prizes for making speeches so I can speak well at meetings. No one else in the class has done this.

Liam

I'm in the football team and swim for the city team. I think we need to improve sports at our school.

- **Fill in the voting slip.** ☒
- **Put it into the ballot box.**

	Josie
	William
	May
	Salim
	Hannah
	Liam

- **Explain your choice.**

_____

_____

_____

_____

Now try this!

- **Write what you think is the most important quality in a class representative.**

Teachers' note This could be used to prepare the children for choosing their class representative for the school council, or it could be used to chitroduce the idea of a school council and to explain how it works. Explain that it is not practical to ask every individual for their opinions about everything that affects the group. Instead, in a democracy, the group chooses a few people to make its decisions. Point out that when people vote in elections they mark their choice with a cross.

Developing Citizenship
Year 4
© **A & C BLACK**

Council problem

How could the school council help these children?

I can never find a peg to hang my coat on.

My sister's coat is always on the dirty cloakroom floor.

What the children can do

_____

_____

_____

_____

↓

What their class's school council representative can do

_____

_____

_____

_____

↓

What could happen next

_____

_____

_____

_____

Now try this!

- **Write about another problem with which a school council could help.**

Teachers' note This activity can be undertaken whether or not the school has a pupil council. If it does not, it will be necessary first to explain how it works. If the school has a pupil council, it might be appropriate first to reflect on its purpose and how it operates. Point out that when a representative is chosen by a class, he or she is being trusted to act and speak on behalf of the others and that this is how democracy works.

Developing Citizenship
Year 4
© **A & C BLACK**

A fizzy question

- **Work with a group.**
- **Discuss this question:**

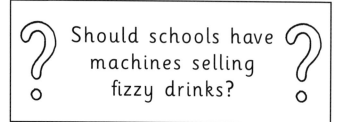

Should schools have machines selling fizzy drinks?

You need

a cassette recorder

a cassette

a stopwatch or timer

You have 10 minutes.

- **Record your discussion.**
- **Vote** | yes | **or** | no | **by a show of hands.**

Result _____

- **Listen to the recording of your discussion.**
- **Complete the chart.**

Reasons for fizzy drinks machines	Reasons against fizzy drinks machines
_____	_____
_____	_____
_____	_____
_____	_____

Number of times each person spoke, and for how long					
Name	Number	Time	Name	Number	Time

Now try this!

- **Write an evaluation of your discussion.**

Teachers' note Tell the children that, in addition to recording their arguments for or against the question under discussion, they are going to consider how well they carried out their discussion. Draw out the main points that make a good discussion: everyone has a chance to speak; the others listen; no one takes over and speaks for too long. This activity sheet is intended to be shared in groups of four.

Developing Citizenship
Year 4
© A & C BLACK

Rules and reasons

Are these rules ⬚sensible⬚ or ⬚silly⬚?

• **Explain your answers.**

Smile at least once a day.	☐	because _____ _____ _____
Keep to the left when walking around the school.	☐	because _____ _____ _____
Count to 100 if you step on an ant.	☐	because _____ _____ _____
Walk to school.	☐	because _____ _____ _____
Ask a question every day.	☐	because _____ _____ _____

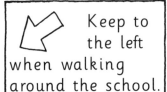

• **Choose one of your school rules.**
• **Explain why it is needed.**

Teachers' note Point out that there are no right answers, although some of the rules could be difficult to keep. Invite feedback after the children have completed the activity. During another lesson, different groups could debate different rules from this page, putting forward their reasons for or against them.

Developing Citizenship
Year 4
© A & C BLACK

Group roles

- **Work with a group.**
- **Plan a five-minute video recording of an interview with a visitor to your school.**
- **Show why this visitor is important.**

Our video should be ready by _____.

- **List the tasks, who will do them and when.**

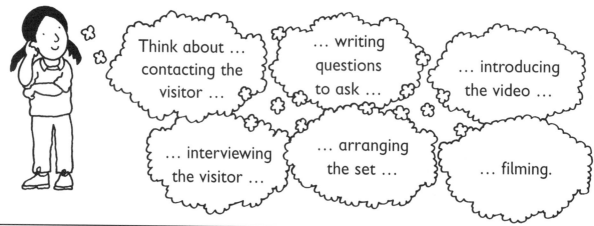

Think about … contacting the visitor …

… writing questions to ask …

… introducing the video …

… interviewing the visitor …

… arranging the set …

… filming.

Task	Who will do it	When

Now try this!

- **Write notes about what you need to do in order to carry out your own task.**

Teachers' note This activity could be linked with any planning in which the children are expected to collaborate in groups. You could mask the project and replace it with another. Give the children a deadline, which they can write in the space provided. Point out that some tasks will take longer than others and that, because of this, some children could take on more than one task. Ask them if they need someone to act as leader (or 'director') for the recording.

Developing Citizenship
Year 4
© A & C BLACK

Yours or ours?

- **Work with a group.**
- **Discuss what should be done in these classrooms.**
- **Write a summary of each discussion.**

Problem

Solution

All the best brushes have gone.

Problem

Solution

We used to have a book on sharks. No one is using it in class, but it isn't here.

SCIENCE

INFORMATION

Problem

Solution

FOOTBALL CUP

SCHOOL PRIZES

The cup has gone!

Now try this!

- **Think about one of the pictures.**

  How did the theft affect the other children?

- **Discuss it with your group.**

Teachers' note Ask the children to think about who owns school property and who is affected when it is stolen. If the property belongs to them, is it stealing if they take it? Draw out that the property belongs to everyone and so everyone should be able to use it. If people keep it for their own use, they are stealing because they keep it from others who have a right to use it.

Developing Citizenship
Year 4
© **A & C BLACK**

Mean burglary

- **Work with a group.**
- **Discuss the causes and effects of this theft.**
- **Underline the key words and phrases.**

TEENAGER LOCKED UP FOR MEAN BURGLARY

A pensioner lost the only photographs she had of her late mother when a teenage burglar raided her home. Disabled Margaret Richardson, 73, had been asleep at the Marsden Rock Nursing Home, South Shields, when Mark Kevin broke in through a bathroom window in the middle of the night.

The 17-year-old fled after grabbing Mrs Richardson's handbag, keeping the £8 cash inside and dumping her treasured photographs, which have not been found. Mrs Richardson raised the alarm after she awoke later in the night to find her bag – placed on her wheelchair next to her bed – had gone missing.

Kevin was traced after his fingerprints were found at the scene. The teenager, of Steward Crescent, South Shields, admitted burglary and was sentenced to 12 months' detention and training. Mr Recorder Dalziel said it was a mean offence and only custody was appropriate.

He said it must have been a frightening experience for Mrs Richardson to learn that an intruder had been next to her bed as she slept.

He told Kevin, "You broke in through a window and got into her room and stole her handbag. It isn't the small sum of money that matters so much, but the only existing photographs of her mother. You threw those away and they have not been recovered."

Rachel Hedworth, defending, said Kevin – who has previous convictions for theft, burglary and handling stolen property – was ashamed of his behaviour, which he described as "horrible". She said the teenager had "gone off the rails" after he and his family had been devastated by the death of his brother, who was killed in an accident two years ago.

Adapted from *Newcastle Evening Chronicle*, 3 September 2004

Now try this!

What do you think about Mark Kevin's punishment?

- **Write about your views.**
- **Support your views with evidence.**

Teachers' note Tell the children that the report they are going to read is a true story from a newspaper. After their discussion, invite feedback and ask them what makes this worse than many other thefts. How do the children feel about Mrs Richardson and Mark Kevin?

Developing Citizenship
Year 4
© A & C BLACK

Putting it right

Many cemeteries have problems with vandalism.

This is what happened to two boys who were caught damaging graves.

- **Answer these questions.**
- **Discuss your answers with a partner.**

Why do you think the youths vandalised graves?

_____

_____

Who are the victims of this crime?

_____

How might the crime affect the victims?

_____

_____

What could be done to help the victims?

_____

_____

What might help the youths to behave better?

_____

_____

Now try this!

- **Find out about other cemetery vandalism.**
- **Write a report about how people are trying to prevent it.**

Teachers' note Ask the children why the boys might have been given such a small fine. If they had very little money, could they have paid a larger fine? What kind of community service would be the most useful for them to be given? The children could consider the ways in which the community service could help to put right the damage the boys caused. They could also investigate the cost of replacing headstones.

Developing Citizenship
Year 4
© A & C BLACK

It's our street

How do people look after your street?

How do people damage your street?

- **Write your observations on the chart.**

Describe actions. Do not write people's names.

Looking after the street	Damaging the street

What can you do to help to care for your street?

⚠️ Do not do anything without permission. Keep off the road. Do not handle litter.

Now try this!

- **Design a competition to encourage people to care for their streets.**
- **Send it to your local council.**

Teachers' note Encourage the children to think about the ways in which people take care of the street where they live (even in small ways): for example, putting litter in bins, planting flowers in gardens or tubs, sweeping up leaves, cleaning up after their dogs. Ask them what kinds of actions by people damage the street: for example, writing graffiti, breaking windows, damaging fences or trees, dropping litter.

54

Developing Citizenship
Year 4
© A & C BLACK

Think about it

- **Work with a group.**
- **Take turns to read a paragraph aloud.**
- **Make a note of your feelings at the end of paragraphs 2, 8, 9, 10 and 12.**

JUST A GAME

1 "Now – let go now!" yelled Gina.

2 "Run!" shouted Kyle. They heard a crash as the trolley landed on the railway. Gasping and panting they dashed from the bridge and through the bushes on the embankment.

3 " Wait! Let's watch and see what happens!" called Terry, still out of breath.

4 "No," said Gina. "Let's get away."

5 Once on the road, they tried to look as if nothing had happened. When Terry got home his mother was on the phone, "I'll try his mobile number again. Maybe there was a delay …"

6 "Where's Dad?" asked Terry.

7 "I'm trying to get him on his mobile," answered his mum. "He had to go to London but he should be back by now."

8 Terry switched on the television. On the news was a report about a train crash. The train had hit a trolley on the line.

9 "That's his train! Dad's on that one!" cried his mum. Terry couldn't speak.

10 Then the phone rang. They didn't want to answer it. His mum took a step towards it. She closed her eyes and picked it up. Then Terry saw tears on her face. She held the phone where he could listen too:

11 "I thought you might be worried – "

12 It was his dad's voice.

What have you learned from this story?

- **Discuss it in your group.**

Now try this!

Which other people could this thoughtless 'game' have affected, and how?

Teachers' note Discuss what made the children in the story throw the trolley on the railway track. The sound of the crashing metal and 'getting away with it' might have excited them. Did they think about the consequences for themselves and others? Do the children think Gina, Kyle and Terry will do this again?

**Developing Citizenship
Year 4**
© A & C BLACK

Landmarks

- **Look for evidence of events from the past in your** [locality]. **You could look at:**

maps

monuments

signs

place names and road names

Evidence	What happened	When

Now try this!

- **Use a computer to design a poster about the history of your locality.**

Teachers' note It would be useful to have a look around the locality first and to plan a route along which to take the children for a walk to look for local landmarks. Others, which are farther afield, could be researched from photographs and information books as well as from maps.

Developing Citizenship Year 4
© A & C BLACK

Past times

- **Find out about the industries in your** $\boxed{\text{locality}}$.
  You could look at the following evidence:

buildings   directories   newspaper advertisements   maps

- **Make a list of local companies.**

Name	Goods or services sold	Date founded

- **Find out about your local industries at a different time in the past.**
- **Make a list of the companies on a copy of the chart.**

Now try this!

- **Write a comparison of the present day and a time in the past in your locality.**

Teachers' note Discuss the meaning of *industry*. Point out that it means all the ways in which people make a living. Focus on those close to the school, some of which the children might not have noticed. For comparison, select a time in the past which is linked with work in history lessons and is particularly relevant for the school's locality.

Developing Citizenship
Year 4
© A & C BLACK

Finding out

- **Find out how the local community has changed.**
- **Plan an interview with an older person who has lived there for a long time.**
- **Write two 'open' questions and two 'closed' questions.**

Questions	Answers

What changes would this person like to see?

_____

_____

What changes would you like to see?

_____

_____

Are there any connections between the changes in your local community?
- **Discuss this with a partner.**

Teachers' note Use this in conjunction with a planned visit by an older member of the local community who is willing to answer the children's questions. Prepare him or her beforehand on the type of questions to expect and encourage the visitor to bring in photographs or other evidence of what the local community was like in the past.

Developing Citizenship
Year 4
© A & C BLACK

Report it

- **Work with a partner.**
- **List the changes you have discovered in your local community.**

Buildings	Industry	Leisure

Shopping	Streets	Transport

- **Choose one topic to find out more about.**
- **Write some questions to help you.**
- **Think about where you can find the answers.**
- **Research the topic and discuss your answers with your partner.**

Now try this!

- **Plan an electronic book about the changes in your local community.**
- **List the different media you will use.**

Teachers' note The children could use as sources of information old and new maps and newspapers, books about the locality and the Internet as well as the results of a survey in which they make sketches, take photographs and make notes about old and new features of the local community. Different pairs could later focus on different aspects of change listed on the chart.

Developing Citizenship
Year 4
© **A & C BLACK**

Factfinder

- **Read the newspaper article with a partner.**

  How does the seller make the lake seem a good buy?

- **Underline the claims he makes.**

- **Circle the claims that can be proved.**

MARINE LAKE UP FOR SALE

By Greg O'Keeffe, *Southport Visiter*

A tourism surge over the next decade will mean that whoever buys Southport's £450,000 marine lake will get a bargain. That is the prediction of current owner Colin Poole, who this week announced he is selling the attraction. The deal includes the double-decker steamer *Southport Belle*, together with 18 speed boats and a lease to operate facilities at Southport Marine Lake and Watersports Centre for the next 11 years.

Mr Poole said, "Potential buyers could revitalise the lake with fresh ideas and imagination. At the moment the town is definitely on the up and there have been a lot of improvements to the sea-front and the lake. I think the Marine Lake is ripe for some new investment and someone who can take advantage of the opportunity. I've been here for years and my future now lies elsewhere. The tourism is the biggest selling point but the Marine Lake is also home to two of the most successful sailing clubs in the country – West Lancashire Yacht Club and Southport Sailing Club. As a complete package I think this is a good price. Behind Pleasureland, the lake is the town's biggest tourism attraction."

The new owner would have to seek permission from Sefton Council before altering the Watersports Centre, Marine Lake or any of the other services. Steve Irwin, sea-front officer and pier master, said: "The council leases the buildings and the lake to Mr Poole, who has now decided to do something else. The council will be involved with the sale up to a point and would vet any potential buyer."

Adapted from *Southport Visiter*, 27 August 2004

- **What kinds of evidence could support the claims?**

- **Record them on a chart.**

  If you wanted to buy the lake, what other information would you check?

Claim	Evidence which could support it	Where to find the evidence

---

Now try this!

- **Re-write the article from the point of view of someone who thinks buying the lake would be a bad idea.**

- **Focus on the problems the buyer might face.**

Teachers' note It is useful to note the alternative spelling of 'visitor' used for the title of this newspaper. You could model how to discuss the passage by reading the first paragraph with the children and pointing out the claim made in the opening sentence (that Southport is at the beginning of a boom in tourism). Discuss what evidence is needed to support this claim.

Developing Citizenship Year 4
© **A & C BLACK**

All sides of the story

- **Find two contrasting reports from different sources about the same story:**

cuttings from newspapers

recordings of radio news programmes

recordings from television news programmes

- **Make notes on the chart.**

Subject of story _____

Source	Facts given	Opinion presented	Evidence for opinion

Now try this!

- **Write a comparison of two different reports of the story.**

Teachers' note Prepare for this activity by choosing an appropriate news story and collecting newspaper cuttings and recordings of radio and television news broadcasts about it. Include some which present different views. Each child could focus on two contrasting reports. Invite feedback to enable them to share what they have discovered.

Developing Citizenship Year 4 © A & C BLACK

A safe place to cross

- **Find out which is the most difficult road to cross in your locality.**

Our group will investigate this road:

_____

- **List the types of evidence you could collect.**

_____

_____

_____

_____

- **Plan an investigation to find out how difficult this road is to cross.**

What we shall do	When
_____	_____
_____	**How often**
_____	_____
_____	_____
How we shall stay safe _____	**Who can help**
_____	_____
_____	_____

Now try this!

- **List the types of evidence that will help you to compare your road with other groups' roads.**
- **Explain how you could use the comparisons.**

Teachers' note This is a group activity with one sheet per group. Ask each group to nominate one road and to say why they have nominated it. What do they mean by 'difficult to cross'? Are there too few crossings or do the traffic lights allow insufficient time for them to cross? Is the traffic travelling too fast? Emphasise the importance of safety in their planning.

**Developing Citizenship
Year 4
© A & C BLACK**

Facts and figures

- **Investigate a difficult road to cross.**
- **Find out how long people have to wait to cross the road.**

Name of road: _____

Place observed: _____

Date: _____

Time: from _____ to _____

 You <u>must</u> have an adult with you.

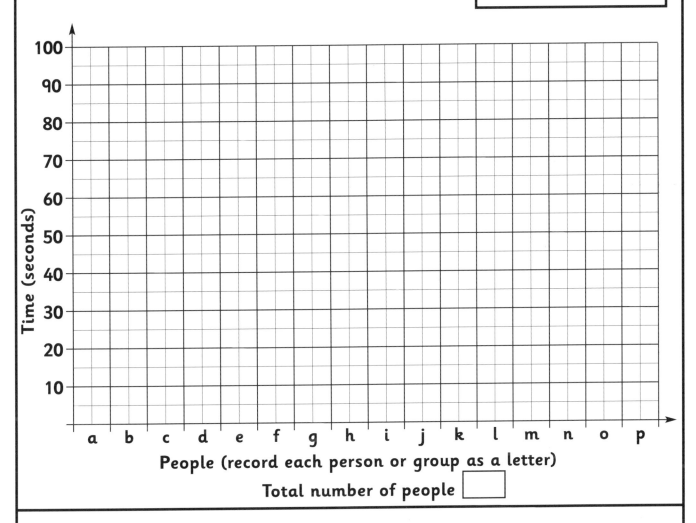

Time (seconds)

100
90
80
70
60
50
40
30
20
10

a b c d e f g h i j k l m n o p

People (record each person or group as a letter)

Total number of people ☐

Now try this!

- **Record any other useful evidence:**

| type of traffic | speed limit |

| pedestrians' views |

Teachers' note This could be used as a follow-up to page 62. Different groups could be taken to different places (under adult supervision) to collect evidence, record their results and then come together to decide which was the most difficult road to cross. Several visits to the same place would increase the reliability of their survey.

Developing Citizenship Year 4
© A & C BLACK

Front page

- ## Write a report about a difficult road to cross.

Get the reader's attention.

Headline _____

Write your name.

by _____

Make it sound interesting. Set the scene.

Opening

_____

_____

Give evidence from your survey.

Facts

_____

_____

_____

Include quotations from pedestrians.

Opinions

_____

_____

_____

Use interesting language. Make your opinion clear.

Summary

_____

Write what your report revealed.

_____

_____

_____

Say what should be done.

_____

Now try this!

- ## Swap reports with a partner.
- ## Edit one another's writing.

Teachers' note This could be used as a follow-up to pages 62–63. Remind the children about what they have learned about the presentation of newspaper reports. Point out that it is acceptable to present opinions but that these need to be supported by evidence. The children might find it easier to write the headline after they have finished the article: it should be eye-catching and summarise what the report is about.

64

**Developing Citizenship
Year 4
© A & C BLACK**